CANON EOS R100- QUICK & CONCISE GUIDE

Modes, Shooting & Setting Processes (Photographer's Quick-Guide Series)

Sam Addy

Table of Contents

The Canon EOS R100 is a compact, mirrorless camera that bridges the gap between entry-level simplicity and professional-grade performance. As one of Canon's most affordable options in the EOS R series, the R100 targets hobbyists, content creators, and budding photographers seeking a balance between portability and capability. With its sleek design, intuitive controls, and a focus on user-friendly functionality, this camera offers an accessible gateway into the world of mirrorless photography.

At the heart of the EOS R100 is a 24.1-megapixel APS-C sensor, which delivers crisp images with vibrant colors and impressive dynamic range. Paired with Canon's renowned Dual Pixel CMOS autofocus system, the camera ensures quick and accurate focusing, even in challenging lighting conditions. This makes it an ideal choice for capturing fast-moving subjects, such as in sports or wildlife photography, and stunning portraits with natural bokeh effects.

One of the standout features of the EOS R100 is its versatility. It supports the RF lens mount system, opening the door to various Canon RF lenses while maintaining compatibility with EF lenses using an adapter. Additionally, its lightweight body makes it perfect for on-the-go creators, from travel photographers to vloggers. With 4K video recording capabilities, the camera caters to videographers who need high-quality footage without the bulk of larger setups.

Despite its compact size and approachable price point, the EOS R100 doesn't shy away from offering advanced features typically found in higher-end models. From wireless connectivity for seamless sharing to customizable shooting modes for creative freedom, the R100 is thoughtfully designed to grow with the user's skills.

The Canon EOS R100 is more than just a camera—it's a tool that empowers creators to capture their vision with confidence. Whether you're stepping into photography for the first time or looking for a capable secondary camera, the R100 promises to deliver quality, convenience, and Canon's trusted reliability.

PURPOSE

This book review aims to provide readers with a comprehensive and unbiased evaluation of the Canon EOS R100, offering insights into its features, performance, and overall value. With the ever-expanding market of mirrorless cameras, choosing the right model can be overwhelming, especially for beginners and hobbyists. This review aims to bridge that gap by breaking down the R100's capabilities, highlighting its strengths, and addressing its limitations in real-world scenarios.

By analyzing the camera from multiple perspectives—design, functionality, performance, and cost-effectiveness—this review seeks to equip potential buyers with the knowledge needed to make an informed decision. Whether you're a photography enthusiast, a travel blogger, or someone exploring vlogging, this review will explore how the R100 aligns with various creative needs and aspirations.

Additionally, this book serves as a resource for users considering upgrading from older DSLRs or compact cameras to a mirrorless system. It will explore how the Canon EOS R100 fits into Canon's broader ecosystem and what sets it apart from its competitors. The review will also help readers understand whether the R100 is the right investment for their photography journey through detailed discussions and real-world examples.

Ultimately, this review is designed to evaluate the Canon EOS R100 and inspire confidence in users seeking to unlock their creative potential. By the end of this review, readers will clearly understand what the R100 offers, who it's best suited for, and how it can enhance their photographic and video-making experiences.

WHO IS THE GUIDE FOR?

The Canon EOS R100 is specifically designed to cater to a wide range of users, from complete beginners to seasoned photographers looking for a lightweight yet capable second camera. Its versatility and user-friendly features make it particularly appealing to the following groups:

1. Beginner Photographers : For those stepping into the world of photography, the EOS R100 is an excellent starting point. Its intuitive controls, built-in guides, and automatic shooting modes simplify the learning process, allowing new users to focus on creativity rather than getting overwhelmed by technicalities.

2. Content Creators and Vloggers : The camera's compact and lightweight design, 4K video recording, and wireless connectivity make it a practical tool for vloggers and content creators. Whether you're shooting travel vlogs, tutorials, or social media content, the R100 provides high-quality results without the burden of a bulky setup.

3. Photography Enthusiasts on a Budget : Aspiring photographers who want to explore the benefits of a mirrorless camera without breaking the bank will find the R100 an ideal choice. Its affordability does not compromise its performance, making it a cost-effective entry point into the EOS R ecosystem.

4. Travelers and On-the-Go Shooters : With its lightweight build and impressive performance in various conditions, the EOS R100 is perfect for travelers and casual shooters. It's small enough to carry everywhere yet powerful enough to capture memorable moments, whether you're exploring a bustling city or a serene landscape.

5. Hobbyists Transitioning to Mirrorless : The R100 offers a smoother transition to the mirrorless world for those upgrading from compact cameras or entry-level DSLRs. Its compatibility with RF and EF lenses ensures flexibility, making it an attractive option for users already invested in the Canon ecosystem.

6. Families and Everyday Users : The Canon EOS R100 is also well-suited for families looking to document everyday moments. Its reliable autofocus and image stabilization features make capturing sharp, high-quality photos and videos of special events, family gatherings, and candid moments easy.

CANON EOS R100 SPOT

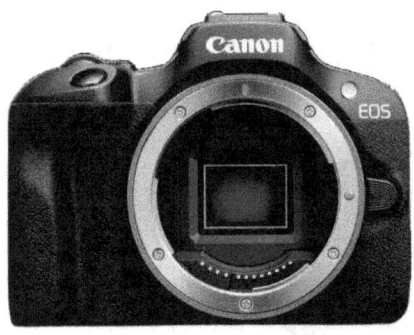
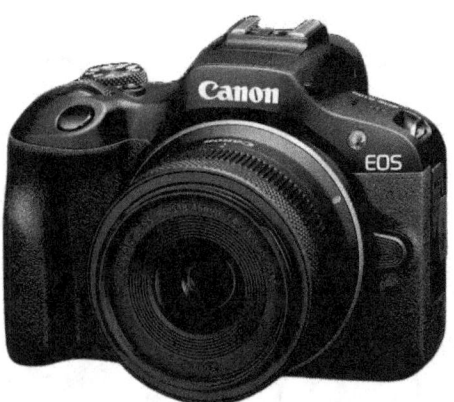
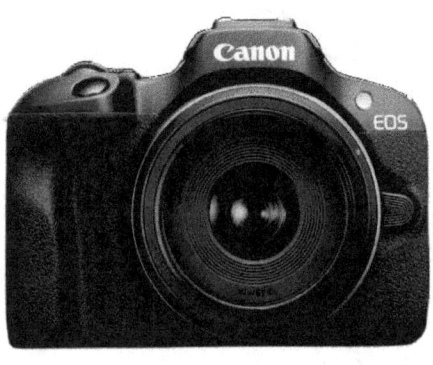
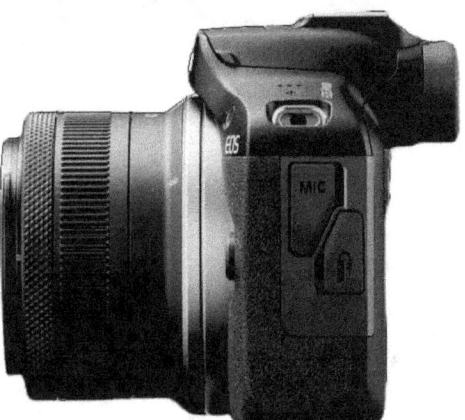
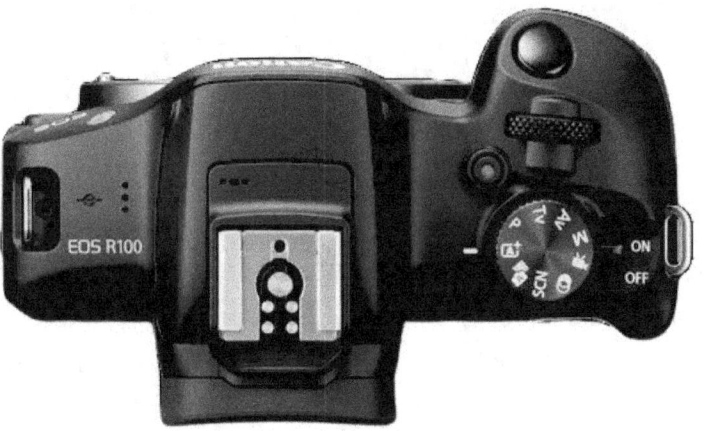

GET FAMILIARIZE

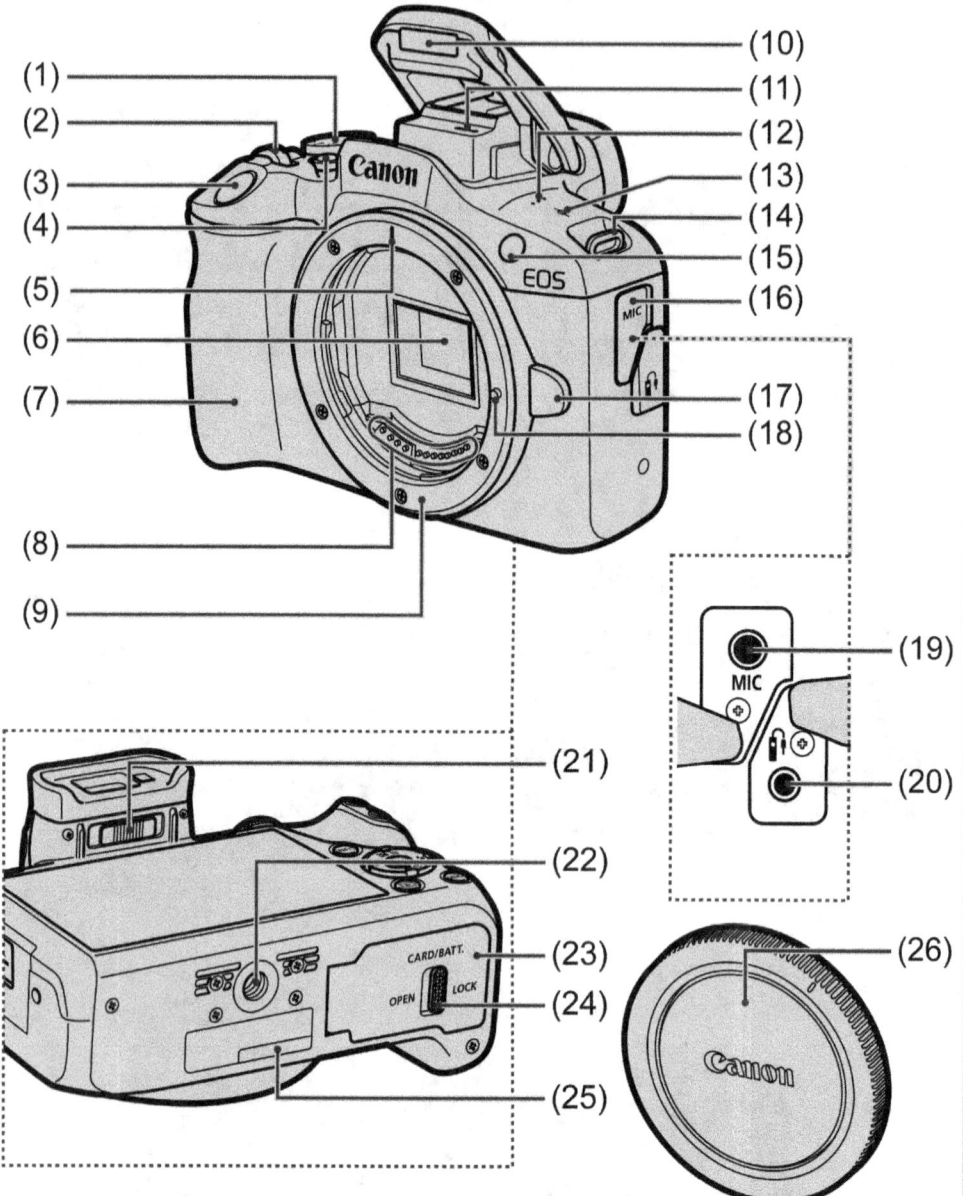

1. Mode Dial: It allows you to select different shooting modes, such as Auto, Manual, Aperture Priority, Shutter Priority, and Scene modes.
2. Dial: Used to adjust settings like shutter speed, aperture, or menu navigation, depending on the mode selected.
3. Shutter Button: Press halfway to focus and fully to take a picture.

4.Movie Shooting Button: A dedicated button to start and stop video recording near the thumb for easy access.

5.RF Lens Mount Index: A red mark on the camera body to align RF lenses when attaching them.

6.Image Sensor: A 24.1MP APS-C CMOS sensor inside the camera body and responsible for capturing light and converting it into digital images.

7.Grip: Ergonomically designed area to comfortably hold the camera.

8.Contacts: Electrical contacts inside the lens mount to communicate between the camera and the attached lens.

9.Lens Mount: The physical connection point on the camera for attaching RF lenses.

10. Built-in Flash: A small, pop-up flash for additional lighting in low-light situations.

11. Microphone (Monaural): Built-in microphone for capturing audio when recording videos.

12. Speaker: For playback of audio during video or image review.

13. Focal Plane Mark: Indicates the exact position of the image sensor, useful for measuring the distance for precise focusing.

14. Strap Mount: Metal loops on either side of the camera for attaching a neck or wrist strap.

15. AF-Assist Beam/Red-Eye Reduction/Self-Timer/Remote Control Lamp: Multi-purpose light assisting with autofocus in low light, reducing red-eye, or acting as a timer or remote signal indicator.

16. Terminal Cover: Protects ports like the HDMI and USB connections from dust and damage.

17. Lens Release Button: Press to detach the lens from the camera body.

18. Lens Lock Pin: Secures the lens to the mount, locking it in place once aligned.

19. External Microphone IN Terminal: A 3.5mm input jack for connecting an external microphone for better audio quality.

20. Remote Control Terminal: Port for connecting a compatible remote control for shutter release or other functions.

21. Dioptric Adjustment Slider: Adjusts the viewfinder focus to match your eyesight.

22. Tripod Socket: Standard threaded mount for attaching the camera to a tripod.

23. Card/Battery Compartment Cover: Protects the slots for the memory card and battery.

24. Card/Battery Compartment Cover Lock: A latch to secure the card/battery compartment cover.

25. Serial Number (Body Number): Unique identification number for the camera body, typically engraved near the battery compartment or bottom plate.

26. Body Cap: Protective cap to cover the lens mount when no lens is attached, preventing dust and damage to the image sensor.

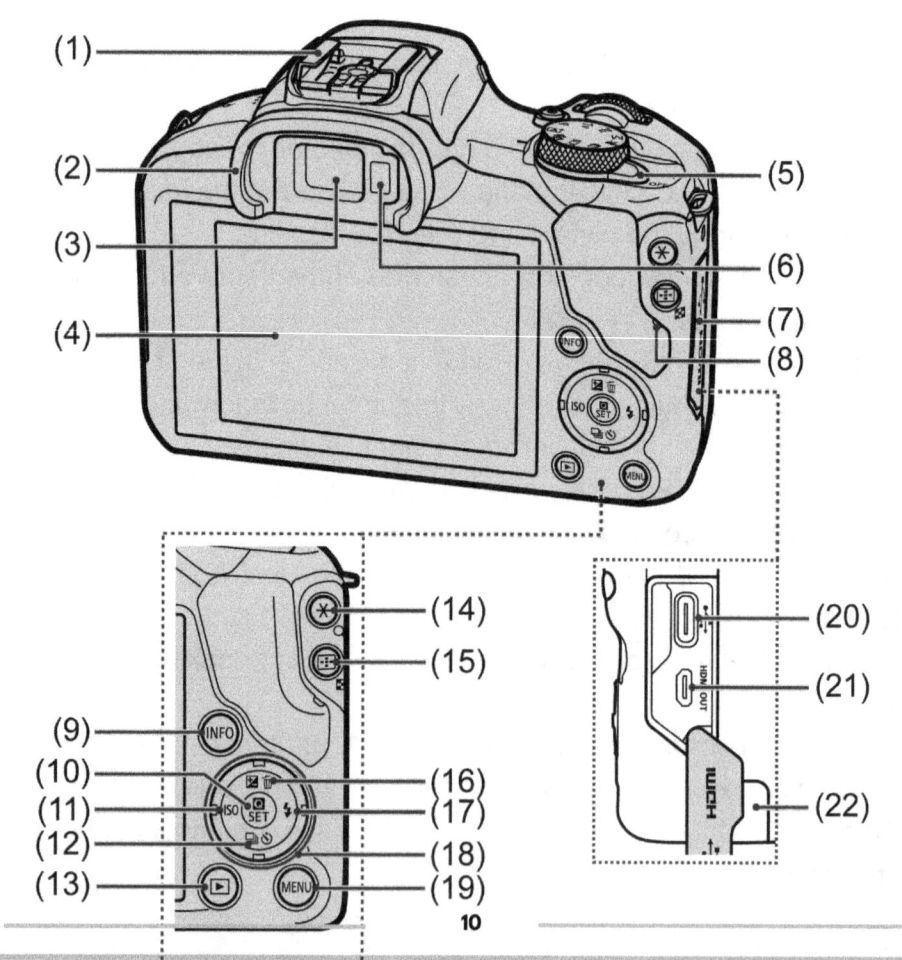

1. Hot Shoe: A metal mount on top of the camera used for attaching external accessories like a flash unit, microphone, or other compatible devices.
2. Eyecup: A soft rubber frame around the viewfinder eyepiece for comfortable viewing and to block stray light.
3. Viewfinder Eyepiece: The optical component through which you can frame and compose your shots directly.
4. Screen: A rear LCD monitor used for live view shooting, navigating menus, reviewing images, or adjusting settings.
5. Power Switch: A toggle or sliding switch to turn the camera on and off.
6. Viewfinder Sensor: Detects when your eye is near the viewfinder to automatically switch from the LCD screen to the electronic viewfinder (if applicable).
7. Terminal Cover: A protective flap that conceals and protects the camera's external connection ports.
8. Access Lamp: Indicates the status of the memory card, such as when it is being written to, read from, or accessed.
9. Info Button: Cycles through different on-screen information displays, such as shooting settings or image details.
10. Quick Control/Set Button: Used to confirm selections and access the Quick Control menu for fast adjustments to shooting settings.
11. Left/ISO Speed Setting Button: Adjusts the ISO sensitivity (light sensitivity) or navigates left in menus.
12. Down/Self-Timer/Drive Mode Selection Button: Allows you to set self-timer options or change drive modes (e.g., single shot, burst mode).
13. Playback Button: Opens the playback mode to review captured images and videos.
14. AE Lock/FE Lock/Magnify Button: Locks the exposure settings (AE) or flash exposure (FE); also used to magnify images during playback.
15. AF Point Selection/Index/Reduce Button: Lets you choose the autofocus point; during playback, it reduces zoom or shows multiple images.

16. Up/Exposure Compensation/Erase Button: Adjusts exposure compensation; in playback mode, it erases selected images or videos.

17. Right/Flash Button: Controls flash options or navigates right in menus.

18. Cross Keys: A set of directional buttons (Up, Down, Left, Right) for navigating menus, selecting settings, or adjusting options.

19. Menu Button: Opens the main menu for camera settings and customization.

20. Digital Terminal: A USB port for transferring images or videos to a computer or charging the camera.

21. HDMI Micro OUT Terminal: Allows you to connect the camera to a TV or monitor via an HDMI cable for viewing photos and videos on a larger screen.

22. DC Cord Hole: A small opening that allows the use of an external power adapter for continuous power supply during extended use.

IMAGE SENSOR OF THE CANON EOS R100

The image sensor is the heart of any digital camera, and the Canon EOS R100 features a robust sensor designed to deliver excellent image quality and performance. Below is an expanded explanation of the sensor's specifications and their significance:

1. Type: 22.3 x 14.9mm CMOS

The Canon EOS R100 has an APS-C-sized CMOS (Complementary Metal-Oxide-Semiconductor) sensor measuring 22.3 x 14.9mm. This sensor size is standard for many entry-level and mid-range cameras, balancing image quality, depth of field control, and cost-effectiveness. The APS-C sensor is smaller than full-frame sensors but still large enough to capture high levels of detail, making it ideal for photographers seeking quality without the bulk or expense of a full-frame system.

2. Effective Pixels: Approx. 24.1 Megapixels

With approximately 24.1 effective megapixels, the EOS R100 delivers sharp, detailed images suitable for various applications. This resolution allows for high-quality prints, extensive cropping flexibility, and clear results even when zooming into an image. The sensor's pixel count ensures that the camera can produce images rich in detail, color, and contrast, catering to beginners and experienced photographers.

3. Total Pixels: Approx. 25.8 Megapixels

The total pixel count of approximately 25.8 megapixels includes the extra pixels surrounding the active image area. These additional pixels enhance image processing and stabilization, ensuring that the final output maximizes image quality while minimizing noise.

4. Aspect Ratio: 3:2

The sensor's native aspect ratio 3:2 mirrors traditional 35mm film photography. This aspect ratio is well-suited for various genres, including landscape, portrait, and street photography, providing a natural and balanced frame that works well for printing and sharing.

5. Low-Pass Filter: None

The absence of a low-pass filter (or anti-aliasing filter) on the Canon EOS R100's sensor is a strategic choice to enhance image sharpness and detail.

While a low-pass filter helps reduce moiré patterns in certain scenarios, its removal ensures that images captured by the R100 are exceptionally crisp, making it ideal for subjects with intricate textures, such as landscapes, fabrics, and architecture.

6. Sensor Cleaning: None

The camera does not include an integrated sensor-cleaning mechanism. Users should take extra precautions to prevent dust or debris from settling on the sensor, especially during lens changes. Regular manual cleaning or professional maintenance may be necessary for optimal performance.

7. Color Filter Type: RGB Primary Color

The sensor employs an RGB Primary Color filter to capture vibrant and accurate colors. This ensures that the photos taken with the EOS R100 are true to life, with rich, natural tones that require minimal post-processing. The RGB filter works seamlessly with Canon's image processing engine to reproduce outstanding color.

8. Sensor Shift-IS: No

The EOS R100 does not feature in-body image stabilization (IBIS) through sensor shift. Instead, stabilization relies on the lenses equipped with optical image stabilization (OIS). While this may not be as versatile as IBIS, Canon's extensive range of RF and EF lenses with OIS provides plenty of options for stabilized shooting, particularly for video and low-light photography.

The Canon EOS R100's image sensor is a cornerstone of its capability, balancing affordability and performance. Its APS-C CMOS design, 24.1-megapixel resolution, and absence of a low-pass filter make it an excellent choice for creators who prioritize sharpness, detail, and vibrant color reproduction. Although it lacks sensor cleaning and in-body stabilization, the camera compensates with a rich ecosystem of compatible lenses and Canon's trusted image quality. This sensor makes the EOS R100 a reliable tool for a wide array of creative applications, from everyday snapshots to professional-grade photography.

IMAGE PROCESSOR OF THE CANON EOS R100: DIGIC 8

The Canon EOS R100 is powered by the DIGIC 8 image processor, a key component that enhances the camera's performance, image quality, and overall functionality. The DIGIC (Digital Imaging Integrated Circuit) series is Canon's proprietary image processing technology, and the DIGIC 8 represents a significant advancement in processing power for cameras in this range. Here's an expanded look at what the DIGIC 8 processor brings to the EOS R100:

1. Efficient Image Processing

With remarkable speed and efficiency, the DIGIC 8 processor is designed to handle high-resolution images, such as the 24.1-megapixel photos produced by the R100's APS-C sensor. It ensures that the camera processes images quickly while maintaining optimal quality. This allows photographers to shoot continuously without experiencing delays in processing or buffering.

2. Improved Autofocus Performance

The DIGIC 8 significantly enhances the camera's autofocus system, enabling faster and more accurate focusing. It powers Canon's Dual Pixel CMOS AF technology, ensuring smooth and precise focus tracking for still photography and video recording. This is especially beneficial for capturing moving subjects or recording dynamic scenes.

3. Enhanced Image Quality

The DIGIC 8 processor produces sharp, vibrant images with excellent detail and minimal noise. Working in tandem with the camera's RGB primary color filter ensures accurate color reproduction and smooth gradations. It also enhances dynamic range, allowing the camera to capture more details in highlights and shadows.

4. Support for 4K Video Recording

One of the standout features of the DIGIC 8 processor is its ability to handle 4K video recording. This includes support for 4K UHD (Ultra High Definition) resolution at 24 frames per second, ensuring crisp, high-quality video output. The processor also enables Canon's 4K Frame Grab feature, allowing users to extract high-resolution still images from video footage.

5. Efficient Noise Reduction

The DIGIC 8 excels at reducing noise, particularly in high ISO settings. This is critical for low-light photography, where grainy images can be a common challenge. The processor's noise reduction algorithms ensure that images retain clarity and detail, even in dimly lit environments.

6. Lens Optimization

The DIGIC 8 works seamlessly with Canon's extensive lineup of RF and EF lenses, supporting advanced features like Digital Lens Optimizer (DLO). DLO corrects optical aberrations, such as distortion and chromatic aberration, directly in-camera, ensuring that each photo achieves optimal sharpness and clarity without requiring extensive post-processing.

7. Real-Time Subject Recognition

The processor enhances the R100's ability to recognize and track subjects in real time, whether they are people, animals, or other objects. This is crucial for focusing on moving subjects and achieving well-composed shots in dynamic situations.

8. Streamlined Workflow

The DIGIC 8 also supports modern connectivity features, such as Wi-Fi and Bluetooth, making transferring images and videos to other devices easier. The processor enables fast image compression and storage, ensuring photographers can manage their workflow efficiently.

LENS SYSTEM

The lens system of the Canon EOS R100 is one of its defining features, offering flexibility and compatibility for various photography and videography needs. Here's a detailed look at its specifications and what they mean for users:

1. Lens Mount: RF

The Canon EOS R100 is built around the RF mount, part of Canon's next-generation lens ecosystem. Introduced with the EOS R series, the RF mount is designed to maximize optical performance, allowing for faster communication between the lens and the camera body. This results in improved autofocus speed, enhanced image quality, and access to advanced features like lens corrections directly in-camera.

2. Compatibility: RF and RF-S (with Adapter Support for EF and EF-S Lenses)

The EOS R100 natively supports Canon's RF and RF-S lenses, providing access to a growing selection of high-quality lenses tailored for full-frame and APS-C cameras. Additionally, users can expand their options by utilizing Canon's mount adapter, which allows full compatibility with EF and EF-S lenses. This backward compatibility is a major advantage for photographers who own EF lenses from Canon's DSLR systems.

Key points of compatibility:

- RF lenses: High-performance lenses with advanced optical designs.
- RF-S lenses: Compact and lightweight lenses designed for APS-C cameras.
- EF/EF-S lenses: Adaptable via a mount adapter, retaining full functionality, including autofocus and image stabilization.
- This compatibility ensures that the EOS R100 provides incredible versatility, catering to new users and long-time Canon enthusiasts.

3. Focal Length: 1.6x Crop Factor

The Canon EOS R100 features an APS-C sensor, which applies a 1.6x crop factor to the focal length of any lens attached. For example:.

- A 50mm lens on the R100 will provide an equivalent focal length of 80mm, making it great for portrait photography.
- A 24mm lens will behave like a 38mm lens, ideal for general-purpose use and street photography.

This crop factor is particularly beneficial for telephoto photography, as it effectively extends the reach of longer lenses, making it a fantastic choice for wildlife and sports photography without requiring excessively long lenses.

4. Image Stabilization (IS): Lens-Based Optical Stabilization

The Canon EOS R100 does not feature in-body image stabilization (IBIS); however, it fully supports optical image stabilization (IS) in lenses equipped with this feature. Lens-based IS minimizes camera shake, resulting in sharper photos and smoother videos, especially in low-light situations or when using long focal lengths.

In addition to optical stabilization, the camera offers Movie Digital IS, which provides enhanced stabilization during video recording. Users can select from the following settings:

- Off: No digital stabilization applied.
- Enabled: Moderate stabilization for handheld shooting.
- Enhanced: Maximum stabilization is ideal for more extreme movements or shooting without a tripod.

The lens-based optical IS and Movie Digital IS make the EOS R100 a solid performer for handheld photography and videography.

FOCUSING SYSTEM

The Canon EOS R100 features an advanced Dual Pixel CMOS AF System that ensures precise, fast, and reliable focusing for still photography and video recording. Here's a comprehensive breakdown of its focusing capabilities:

1. Type: Dual Pixel CMOS AF System

The Dual Pixel CMOS AF System is Canon's proprietary autofocus technology, designed to provide phase-detection autofocus on the image sensor. This system delivers smooth and accurate focusing by using nearly every pixel on the sensor for focus detection. It ensures:

- Fast focusing speed is crucial for capturing action shots or fleeting moments.
- Smooth transitions, particularly for video, eliminate abrupt or jerky focus shifts.
- Accurate subject tracking, ideal for both photography and videography.

However, during 4K Movie Servo AF, the system uses a contrast detection method instead, which may result in slightly slower focus acquisition in 4K video mode.

2. Maximum AF Zones (Stills / Movies): 143 / 117

The EOS R100 divides its sensor into 143 autofocus zones for stills and 117 for video, providing wide frame coverage. This ensures that subjects can be tracked and focused on effectively, even at the edges of the image.

3. AF System/Points

- Stills: Up to 3,975 AF positions are available for manual selection, offering granular control over focus placement.
- Movies: Up to 3,375 AF positions ensure flexibility during video recording.
- Face+Tracking Mode: In automatic mode, the camera can select up to 143 points (stills) or 99 points (movies) to seamlessly track subjects like faces or eyes.

- Zone AF: In Zone AF mode, users can select from 25 zones, simplifying the process of focusing on specific areas of the frame

4. AF Working Range: EV -4 to 18 (Stills) / EV -2 to 18 (Movies)

The EOS R100 performs well in various lighting conditions, with an AF working range of EV -4 to 18 for stills and EV -2 to 18 for movies. This lets the camera focus accurately even in low-light situations, such as dimly lit interiors or night scenes, ensuring sharp and clear results.

5. AF Modes

- One-Shot AF: Ideal for still subjects, where the focus is locked after achieving focus.
- Servo AF: Continuously tracks and adjusts focus for moving subjects, ensuring sharpness even with dynamic motion.

6. AF Point Selection

The EOS R100 offers multiple options for selecting autofocus points:

- Face+Tracking: Automatically detects and focuses on human faces, eyes, heads, or bodies, making it perfect for portraits or video interviews.
- Spot AF: Focuses on a very small, precise area of the frame.
- 1-Point AF: Allows for a more targeted focus on a single point in the frame.
- Zone AF: Divides the frame into zones, giving more control for larger or dynamic subjects.
- Manual Selection: Users can freely position a single AF point or zone, depending on the lens and shooting situation.

7. AF Tracking

The camera's AF tracking is tailored to track human subjects effectively, focusing on:

- Eyes: Ensures sharp focus on the subject's eyes, which is critical for portraits.
- Face: Detects and locks onto faces for reliable tracking.
- Head: Maintains focus on a subject's head, even if the face isn't fully visible.

- Body: Tracks the subject's body for broader movement scenarios.

8. AF Lock

Focus can be locked by:
- Half-pressing the shutter button: Ensures the subject stays focused while composing the shot.
- Customizable AF Lock Button: Offers flexibility to assign AF lock to other buttons, depending on user preferences.

9. AF Assist Beam

The EOS R100 includes an LED assist beam for low-light scenarios, helping the autofocus system acquire focus more effectively when lighting conditions are challenging.

10. Manual Focus (MF)

The camera provides robust manual focus options:
- With RF Lenses: Dedicated AF/MF switch on the lens or via menu settings.
- With EF/EF-S Lenses: Use the AF/MF switch on the lens itself.
- MF Peaking: Highlights the in-focus areas with colored outlines, making manual focus adjustments more precise.
- AF+MF allows manual focus adjustment after the autofocus locks on a subject, combining the best of both worlds.
- Magnify Image: Users can magnify the view by 3-10x in 0.1x increments, ensuring pinpoint accuracy for fine adjustments.

11. Focus Bracketing

The EOS R100 does not provide focus bracketing, a feature that allows users to capture multiple images at different focus distances for stacking later in post-processing.

EXPOSURE CONTROL

The Canon EOS R100 is equipped with a versatile and advanced exposure control system, ensuring accurate and consistent results in a variety of lighting conditions. Here's an expanded look at its key features:

1. Metering Modes
The EOS R100 uses real-time metering from the image sensor, offering four different metering modes to suit various shooting scenarios:
- Evaluative Metering (384 zones, 24x16): This is the default mode, using 384 zones to analyze the entire scene. It provides a balanced exposure by considering factors like subject brightness, contrast, and position, making it ideal for most situations.
- Partial Metering (approx. 5.8% of the Live View screen): Useful for backlit or high-contrast scenes, this mode measures a small area around the center of the frame, ensuring accurate exposure for the subject. (Stills only)
- Center-Weighted Average Metering: This mode places emphasis on the center of the frame while considering the entire scene for an average exposure, making it suitable for portraits and scenarios with a well-lit central subject.
- Spot Metering (approx. 2.9% of the Live View screen): The most precise metering mode, spot metering measures a small, specific area of the frame. This is perfect for high-contrast scenes where you want to ensure proper exposure for a particular subject. (Stills only)
- Note: Partial and spot metering are not available in movie mode.

2. Metering Brightness Range
The EOS R100 offers a wide metering brightness range:
- Still Images: EV -2 to 20, allowing accurate metering even in low-light conditions or high-contrast scenarios.
- Movies: EV 0 to 20, ensuring consistent exposure when recording videos in a variety of lighting environments.
- This range enhances the camera's flexibility, making it suitable for both indoor and outdoor shooting, day or night.

3. AE Lock (Auto Exposure Lock)

The camera offers two options for locking exposure:

- Auto AE Lock: In One-shot AF mode, the exposure is locked automatically as soon as the subject is in focus. This ensures consistent exposure while recomposing the shot.
- Manual AE Lock: By pressing the AE Lock button, users can lock the exposure in creative modes or during movie recording. This provides greater control in challenging lighting conditions, such as when shooting against bright backdrops.

4. Exposure Compensation

The EOS R100 supports exposure compensation of +/-3 EV in 1/3-stop increments. This feature is crucial for adjusting the brightness of an image manually, especially in scenes with tricky lighting, such as backlit subjects or high-contrast environments. Exposure compensation ensures that photographers can achieve the desired brightness and mood in their photos.

5. Auto Exposure Bracketing (AEB)

The camera offers AEB with 3 shots and a range of +/- 2 EV in 1/3-stop increments. AEB is an essential feature for HDR photography or challenging lighting scenarios, as it captures three images at different exposure levels:

- One at the metered exposure.
- One underexposed.
- One overexposed.

This allows photographers to choose the best exposure or blend the images in post-processing for a balanced result.

6. Anti-Flicker Shooting

The EOS R100 features anti-flicker detection, which compensates for flickering light sources, such as fluorescent or LED lights operating at frequencies of 100Hz or 120Hz. This ensures consistent exposure and color balance when shooting in environments with artificial lighting. However, high-frequency anti-flicker shooting is not provided.

7. ISO Sensitivity

The ISO sensitivity range of the EOS R100 provides excellent flexibility for capturing images in various lighting conditions:

- Normal ISO Range: ISO 100–12,800, adjustable in 1/3 or 1-stop increments. This range is suitable for most scenarios, from bright outdoor environments to moderately low light.
- Expanded ISO: ISO H (equivalent to ISO 25,600) is available for extremely low-light situations. While higher ISO levels may introduce some noise, the camera's DIGIC 8 processor helps to minimize it, delivering usable results in challenging lighting.

SHUTTER SYSTEM

The shutter mechanism of the Canon EOS R100 plays a critical role in controlling exposure and achieving the desired results in various shooting scenarios. Below is a detailed breakdown of its shutter system and features:

1. Shutter Type

The EOS R100 employs an electronically controlled focal-plane shutter, which uses the image sensor to regulate the shutter mechanism. This system combines the following elements:

- Electronic First Curtain: The initial part of the exposure is controlled electronically, reducing mechanical wear and vibrations.
- Mechanical Second Curtain: The second part of the exposure is controlled mechanically, ensuring consistent and reliable operation.
- This hybrid system balances speed, durability, and precision while minimizing potential image distortion caused by vibrations.

2. Shutter Speed

The camera offers a versatile shutter speed range to accommodate a variety of creative and technical needs:

- Standard Range: 30 seconds to 1/4000 second, adjustable in 1/3-stop increments. This range is suitable for most scenarios, including:

    Long exposures for night photography or light trails.

    Fast shutter speeds to freeze motion, such as in sports or wildlife photography.
- Bulb Mode: Allows the shutter to remain open as long as the shutter button is pressed, ideal for capturing extremely long exposures, such as star trails or low-light scenes.

Note: The available shutter speed range may vary depending on the selected shooting mode (e.g., manual, aperture priority, or shutter priority).

3. Rolling Shutter

The EOS R100 utilizes a rolling shutter mechanism when operating with its electronic shutter. While rolling shutters enable faster readouts

, they may introduce slight distortions (e.g., skewed lines) in fast-moving subjects or during panning. However, for most casual and semi-professional use cases, this is rarely noticeable.

4. Shutter Release

The soft-touch electromagnetic release ensures a smooth and responsive shutter operation. This design reduces vibrations caused by pressing the shutter button, minimizing the risk of motion blur in handheld shooting. It enhances the overall user experience by providing a tactile yet silent response, making it ideal for environments where discretion is necessary, such as during events or in quiet settings.

Applications and Benefits

- Fast Shutter Speeds: Perfect for capturing high-speed action like sports or wildlife.
- Long Exposures: Great for creative effects like light trails, silky waterfalls, or astrophotography.
- Hybrid Shutter System: Combines the benefits of electronic and mechanical components for reliability and precision.
- Silent Operation: The soft-touch release minimizes noise and vibration, making it suitable for candid photography or shooting in quiet environments.

WHITE BALANCE SYSTEM

The white balance (WB) system of the Canon EOS R100 is designed to ensure accurate color representation under various lighting conditions. It provides both automatic and manual options for users to achieve the desired color tone in their photos and videos. Below is an in-depth look at its white balance features:

1. White Balance Type

The Canon EOS R100 uses Auto White Balance (AWB) powered by the imaging sensor, which analyzes the scene to automatically determine the appropriate color balance. This ensures that images have natural and accurate colors, regardless of the lighting conditions.

2. White Balance Settings

The EOS R100 offers a variety of pre-set and customizable white balance options, catering to different lighting scenarios and creative needs. The settings include:

- AWB (Ambience Priority): Preserves the warm tones of ambient light for a natural, cozy feel.
- AWB (White Priority): Neutralizes the color cast for pure whites, especially under artificial lighting.
- Daylight: Ideal for outdoor photography under bright sunlight.
- Shade: Warms up the image to compensate for the cooler tones in shaded areas.
- Cloudy: Adds warmth to images taken under overcast skies.
- Tungsten Light: Adjusts for the yellowish-orange tones of indoor tungsten lighting.
- White Fluorescent Light: Corrects the greenish tint often found under fluorescent lighting.
- Flash: Optimized for images taken with a camera flash.
- Custom: Allows users to set a custom white balance by selecting a reference image or using a gray card.
- Color Temperature Setting: Enables manual adjustment of the color temperature in Kelvin for precise control.

3. White Balance Compensation

The camera provides fine-tuning for white balance, allowing users to adjust color tones to their preference. This feature is especially useful for achieving more accurate results in challenging lighting conditions:

- Blue/Amber Adjustment: +/-9 levels.
- Magenta/Green Adjustment: +/-9 levels.

These adjustments give users control over subtle shifts in color tone, ensuring precise customization to match their creative vision.

4. White Balance Shift

The WB Shift feature enables further refinement of white balance settings, with adjustments available in:

- Blue/Amber: +/-9 levels, to add cooler (blue) or warmer (amber) tones.
- Magenta/Green: +/-9 levels, to compensate for magenta or green color casts.

This level of control ensures that photographers can fine-tune their white balance to match the specific lighting environment or achieve a particular artistic effect.

5. Custom White Balance

The EOS R100 supports custom white balance, which allows users to create a personalized WB setting based on a reference image. This is particularly useful for achieving accurate colors in mixed lighting environments or when shooting with unique light sources. The process involves selecting an image from the camera's memory card to serve as the white balance reference.

6. White Balance Bracketing (WB Bracketing)

The camera includes WB Bracketing, which captures multiple images with varying white balance settings to ensure the best result:

- Adjustment Range: +/-3 levels, in single-level increments. This feature is ideal for situations where lighting conditions are unpredictable or when photographers want to experiment with different color tones in post-processing.

Practical Applications

1. Automatic Modes: Ideal for beginners and general shooting scenarios, where the camera intelligently adjusts white balance for natural results.
2. Preset Modes: Useful for quickly adapting to common lighting conditions like daylight, shade, or fluorescent lighting.
3. Custom WB and WB Bracketing: Essential for advanced users who want full control over color accuracy in challenging or mixed lighting environments.

The viewfinder of the Canon EOS R100 is a critical component that enhances the shooting experience, providing photographers with precise framing and real-time information. Below is a detailed explanation of the viewfinder's features and functionalities:

1. Type: 0.39-Type OLED Electronic Viewfinder

The EOS R100 features a 0.39-inch OLED electronic viewfinder (EVF), which provides a bright, high-contrast, and clear display. OLED technology ensures excellent color reproduction, sharp details, and minimal lag, making it ideal for still photography and video recording.

2. Dot Count: Approx. 2,360,000 Dots

The EVF boasts a resolution of approximately 2.36 million dots, delivering a sharp and detailed view. This high resolution allows photographers to:

- Assess focus accuracy.
- Preview the effects of settings like exposure, white balance, and depth of field.
- Compose shots with confidence, even in challenging lighting conditions.

3. Coverage (Vertical/Horizontal): Approx. 100%

The viewfinder offers approximately 100% coverage, ensuring that what you see in the viewfinder matches exactly what will be captured in the final image. This is particularly useful for precise framing, reducing the need for cropping in post-processing.

4. Magnification: Approx. 0.95x

With a magnification of approximately 0.95x, the EVF provides a natural and immersive viewing experience. This level of magnification ensures that subjects appear large and clear, making it easier to focus and compose shots accurately.

5. Eyepoint: Approx. 22mm

The eyepoint of approximately 22mm provides a comfortable viewing experience, even for users wearing glasses. This ensures that the entire frame is visible without adjusting your eye position.

6. Dioptre Correction: Approx. -3.0 to +1.0 m-1 (dpt)

The built-in dioptre adjustment allows users to fine-tune the viewfinder's focus to match their vision, eliminating the need for corrective lenses while using the EVF. The range of -3.0 to +1.0 m-1 accommodates a variety of visual needs.

7. Viewfinder Information

The EVF provides extensive real-time information to assist photographers:

- Viewfinder Sensor: Automatically activates the EVF when the camera detects the presence of your eye, conserving battery life when not in use.
- Vertical Display: Available for still photography, making it easier to compose shots in portrait orientation.
- Exposure Simulation: Allows users to preview how exposure settings affect the final image in real-time.
- Customizable Information Display: The viewfinder's display can be toggled and customized via the [INFO] button, offering three modes:

(1) Liveview image with exposure info.

(2) Liveview image with basic info.

(3) Liveview image with full info.

- Additional Features:

  Grid Overlay: Choose from three formats to assist with composition.

  Histogram: View brightness or RGB histograms to analyze tonal distribution.

  Viewfinder Brightness: Manually adjustable across five levels to adapt to different lighting conditions.

8. Depth of Field Preview: Yes

The EOS R100 includes a depth of field preview function, allowing photographers to see how aperture settings will affect the depth of field before capturing the image. This feature is particularly useful for landscape and macro photography, where precise depth control is crucial.

9. Eyepiece Shutter: No

The camera does not include an eyepiece shutter, meaning there's no built-in mechanism to block stray light from entering the viewfinder during long exposures or when the camera is mounted on a tripod.

Applications and Benefits

- Real-Time Feedback: The electronic viewfinder provides real-time adjustments for exposure, white balance, and focus, helping users achieve their desired results effortlessly.
- Comfortable Viewing: High-resolution, customizable display options and dioptre correction ensure a comfortable and efficient shooting experience.
- Creative Tools: Features like grid overlays and histograms allow photographers to fine-tune their compositions and achieve professional results.

LCD MONITOR

The LCD monitor of the Canon EOS R100 is a vital component for reviewing images, navigating the menu, and composing shots when not using the viewfinder. Here's an in-depth look at its features and functionality:

1. Type
The EOS R100 features a 7.5 cm (3.0-inch) LCD screen with the following specifications:
- TFT (Thin Film Transistor) technology: Provides clear and bright visuals with accurate color reproduction.
- Aspect Ratio: 3:2, matching the sensor's native aspect ratio for optimal image display without cropping.
- Resolution: Approx. 1,040,000 dots, delivering sharp, detailed visuals for composing, reviewing images, and navigating the menu.

2. Coverage
The LCD offers approximately 100% coverage, ensuring that what you see on the screen corresponds exactly to the captured image. This is particularly useful for precise framing and checking the composition.

3. Brightness Adjustment
The LCD monitor's brightness can be adjusted to one of seven levels, allowing users to adapt the display to various lighting conditions:
- Higher brightness: Ideal for outdoor shooting in bright sunlight.
- Lower brightness: Reduces glare in low-light environments, conserving battery life.

4. Touch Screen Operations
The EOS R100 does not feature touch screen functionality, which may require users to rely on physical buttons and dials for menu navigation and settings adjustments. While this simplifies the design, it may feel less intuitive for users accustomed to touch interfaces.

5. Display Options

The LCD provides customizable display modes to suit different shooting needs. Users can toggle between these modes using the [INFO] button:

(1) Liveview Image with Exposure Info: Displays the image along with critical exposure details.

(2) Liveview Image with Basic Info: Shows the image with minimal information for an uncluttered view.

(3) Liveview Image with Full Info: Includes detailed shooting settings and data, ideal for photographers who need comprehensive control over their shots.

6. Customizable Settings

To further enhance usability, the LCD offers the following custom settings:

- Grid Overlay: Three formats are available to aid in composition and alignment, such as for rule-of-thirds or architectural photography.
- Histogram: Provides both brightness and RGB histograms for evaluating tonal distribution and color balance in real-time.

Applications and Benefits

1. Precise Framing and Composition: The 100% coverage ensures that what you see on the screen is exactly what will appear in your final image.
2. Adaptability to Lighting: With seven levels of brightness adjustment, the LCD performs well in both bright outdoor conditions and dim indoor settings.
3. Information at a Glance: The customizable display options allow photographers to view as much or as little shooting information as needed, improving workflow and convenience.
4. Enhanced Composition Tools: The grid overlay and histogram features help photographers fine-tune their shots for better composition and exposure.

FLASH SYSTEM

The Canon EOS R100 features a capable flash system that enhances low-light shooting and creative lighting options. Below is a detailed explanation of its built-in and external flash capabilities:

1. Built-in Flash Specifications
- Guide Number (GN): The built-in flash has a guide number of 6 (ISO 100, meters), indicating its light output. This is suitable for close-range photography, such as portraits or indoor settings.
- Coverage: The built-in flash covers approximately 18mm angle of view, making it effective for wide-angle shots. This coverage corresponds to an 18mm lens on an APS-C sensor, ensuring uniform lighting across the frame.
- Recycle Time: The flash takes approximately 5 seconds to recharge after firing, allowing for relatively quick consecutive shots.

2. Flash Modes
The EOS R100 offers a range of flash modes to suit various shooting conditions:
- Auto: The flash fires automatically when needed, such as in low light or backlit scenarios.
- Fire: Forces the flash to fire in every shot, regardless of lighting conditions.
- Off: Disables the flash completely.
- E-TTL II Flash Metering: The camera uses Canon's Evaluative Through-The-Lens (E-TTL II) flash metering system for optimal exposure. The metering modes include:
Evaluative (Face Priority): Prioritizes proper exposure for detected faces.
Evaluative: Considers the entire scene for balanced flash output.
Average: Averages the exposure across the entire frame.

3. Additional Built-in Flash Features
- Red-Eye Reduction: Helps reduce red-eye effects in portraits by using a pre-flash to constrict pupils.

- X-Sync Speed: The flash syncs at a maximum shutter speed of 1/250 sec, allowing for clear images when combining flash with ambient light.
- Flash Exposure Compensation: Provides +/- 2 EV adjustment in 1/3 increments, giving users precise control over flash brightness to achieve the desired exposure.
- Flash Exposure Lock: Locks the flash exposure to ensure consistent results across multiple shots.
- Second Curtain Synchronization: Enables the flash to fire at the end of the exposure, creating natural-looking motion trails in long-exposure shots.

4. External Flash Compatibility

The EOS R100 supports external flashes for more advanced lighting setups:

- Multi-Function Hot Shoe: The camera includes a 5-pin shoe for mounting external flash units.
- Compatibility: Fully compatible with Canon's EX and EL series Speedlites, offering support for E-TTL II metering. Wireless multi-flash setups are also supported for more creative lighting arrangements.
- Control: External flashes can be controlled directly from the camera's Flash Setting Menu, providing seamless integration and ease of use.

5. Flash Limitations

- Flash Exposure Bracketing: The camera does not support flash exposure bracketing, which could be a limitation for users who rely on multiple exposure levels for advanced lighting techniques.
- Power Output: The built-in flash is not powerful enough for distant subjects or large scenes, requiring an external flash for more demanding applications.

Applications and Benefits

1. Portrait Photography: The built-in flash is effective for close-range portraits, with features like red-eye reduction enhancing results.
2. Low-light Shooting: Provides adequate illumination for indoor and nighttime photography.
3. Creative Lighting: Features like second curtain synchronization and external flash compatibility enable creative effects and advanced setups.
4. Wireless Flash Control: External flash units can be used wirelessly, opening up possibilities for professional-grade lighting.

SHOOTING CAPABILITIES

The Canon EOS R100 offers a variety of shooting modes and features to cater to photographers and videographers of all skill levels. Below is a comprehensive breakdown of its shooting capabilities:

1. Shooting Modes: Stills
The R100 includes a wide range of shooting modes to accommodate various scenarios, from automatic options for beginners to manual settings for advanced users.

1. Scene Intelligent Auto: A fully automatic mode where the camera analyzes the scene and selects the optimal settings, perfect for beginners.
2. Hybrid Auto: Combines stills with a short video clip before each shot, creating a dynamic visual summary of the day.
3. SCN Special Scene Modes: Offers 10 preset modes tailored to specific shooting conditions:

Portrait: Optimized for skin tones and background blur.

Landscape: Enhances depth of field and vivid colors.

Sports: Captures fast-moving subjects with high shutter speeds.

Panning: Keeps moving subjects sharp while blurring the background for dynamic motion effects.

Close-up: Ideal for macro shots with enhanced detail.

Food: Enhances colors and textures for appealing food photography.

Night Portrait: Balances flash and ambient light for natural night shots.

Handheld Night Scene: Reduces motion blur in low light without a tripod.

HDR Backlight Control: Merges multiple exposures for balanced lighting in high-contrast scenes.

Silent Shutter Mode: Reduces shutter noise, ideal for quiet environments.

- Creative Filters: Add artistic effects directly in-camera, with options like:

Grainy B/W: Creates a high-contrast monochrome look.

Soft Focus: Produces a dreamy, softened image.

Fish-eye Effect: Simulates the distortion of a fisheye lens.

Water Painting Effect: Gives images a painterly look.

Toy Camera Effect: Adds vignetting and color tones for a retro aesthetic.

Miniature Effect: Blurs parts of the image to mimic a tilt-shift lens.

HDR Art Modes: Four styles (Standard, Vivid, Bold, Embossed) for high-dynamic-range effects.

- Advanced Shooting Modes:

P (Program AE): Automatic mode with flexibility for certain adjustments.

Tv (Shutter-Priority AE): User sets the shutter speed, and the camera adjusts aperture.

Av (Aperture-Priority AE): User sets the aperture, and the camera adjusts shutter speed.

M (Manual Exposure): Full manual control of both shutter speed and aperture, including bulb mode for long exposures.

2. Shooting Modes: Movies

- Movie Auto Exposure: Automatically adjusts exposure settings for video recording, simplifying the process for beginners.
- Movie Manual Exposure: Offers full control over shutter speed, aperture, and ISO for experienced videographers.

3. Picture Styles

The camera provides customizable picture styles to adjust the tone and color of images:

- Auto, Standard, Portrait, Landscape, Fine Detail, Neutral, Faithful, Monochrome.
- User Defined (x3): Save and customize personal presets.

4. Color Space

- sRGB: Standard color space for general use.
- Adobe RGB: Ideal for professional workflows requiring a wider color gamut.

5. Image Processing Features

- Highlight Tone Priority: Enhances detail in highlights, available in standard and enhanced modes.
- Auto Lighting Optimizer: Adjusts brightness and contrast, with four intensity levels.
- Noise Reduction:

Long Exposure Noise Reduction: Reduces noise in long-exposure shots.

High ISO Noise Reduction: Four settings plus Multi-Shot NR for cleaner images in low light.

- Lens Corrections:

Lens Peripheral Illumination Correction: Fixes vignetting.

Chromatic Aberration Correction: Reduces color fringing.

Diffraction Correction: Enhances sharpness in high aperture settings.

Digital Lens Optimizer (DLO): Corrects multiple optical distortions for supported lenses.

6. Creative Assist

- Presets: Quickly apply pre-configured settings for different looks.
- Adjustments:

Background Blur (5 settings).

Brightness (19 levels).

Contrast (9 levels).

Saturation (9 levels).

Color Tone 1 & 2 (19 levels each).

Monochrome Options: Off/Black and White/Sepia/Blue/Purple/Green.

7. Drive Modes

The camera provides flexible drive options for different shooting needs:

- Single Shooting: Captures one image at a time.
- Continuous Shooting:

One Shot AF: Maximum 6.5 shots/second with electronic first-curtain shutter, capable of capturing up to 97 JPEGs or 6 RAW images in one burst.

Servo AF: Maximum 3.5 shots/second, ideal for tracking moving subjects.

- Self-Timer:
  10-second or 2-second delay.
  Continuous shooting with the self-timer.

8. Continuous Shooting

- One Shot AF: Max 6.5 shots/sec, maintaining speed for:
  97 JPEGs (all sizes).
  6 RAW or 17 C-RAW images.
  RAW + JPEG (6 images).
  C-RAW + JPEG (13 images).
- Servo AF: Max 3.5 shots/sec, ensuring sharp focus on moving subjects.

9. Interval Timer

The EOS R100 does not feature an interval timer, which may limit time-lapse capabilities.

Applications and Benefits

1. Versatile Shooting Modes: Ideal for beginners and advanced users alike, with automatic and manual options.
2. Creative Filters and Assist: Enhance creativity with in-camera effects and simplified adjustments.
3. Fast Continuous Shooting: Captures action-packed moments with high-speed burst shooting.
4. Advanced Image Processing: Ensures optimal results with features like noise reduction, lens corrections, and highlight tone priority.

FILE TYPE AND IMAGE SETTINGS

The Canon EOS R100 offers a variety of file types, resolutions, and recording options to suit different photography needs, from casual shooting to professional workflows. Here's a comprehensive breakdown of its file type capabilities:

1. Still Image Type

The EOS R100 supports two main still image formats, catering to both casual photographers and advanced users who require maximum flexibility:

- JPEG:
  8-bit format with two compression options: Standard and Fine.
  Compliant with Exif 2.31 and the Design Rule for Camera File System (DCF) 2.0 standards, ensuring compatibility with most photo editing software and devices.
- RAW:
  High-quality, uncompressed image format offering 14-bit color depth, suitable for professional-grade post-processing.
  Includes C-RAW (Compressed RAW), which retains high image quality with reduced file sizes, saving storage space.
- DPOF Version 1.1 Compliant:
  Allows users to add printing instructions directly to images, such as print quantity or layout, for direct printing from compatible devices.

2. RAW + JPEG Simultaneous Recording

The camera supports simultaneous RAW and JPEG recording, enabling users to save one high-quality RAW file alongside a smaller, easily shareable JPEG. The JPEG can be recorded in any of the available compression levels, providing flexibility for storage and sharing.

3. Image Size Options

The EOS R100 offers multiple resolutions across different aspect ratios, allowing photographers to tailor their image size for specific purposes, including large prints or web uploads.

- RAW/C-RAW:

24.0 Megapixels (6000 x 4000): Full-resolution, ideal for editing and large prints.

- JPEG (3:2 Aspect Ratio): Matches the sensor's native aspect ratio.

  L (Large): 24 megapixels (6000 x 4000).

  M (Medium): 10.6 megapixels (3984 x 2656).

  S1 (Small 1): 5.9 megapixels (2976 x 1984).

  S2 (Small 2): 3.8 megapixels (2400 x 1600).

- JPEG (4:3 Aspect Ratio): Suitable for print and social media with a slightly squarer crop.

  L: 21.3 megapixels (5328 x 4000).

  M: 9.5 megapixels (3552 x 2664).

  S1: 5.3 megapixels (2656 x 1992).

  S2: 3.4 megapixels (2112 x 1600).

- JPEG (16:9 Aspect Ratio): Ideal for widescreen displays and video thumbnails.

  L: 20.2 megapixels (6000 x 3368).

  M: 8.9 megapixels (3984 x 2240).

  S1: 5.0 megapixels (2976 x 1680).

  S2: 3.2 megapixels (2400 x 1344).

- JPEG (1:1 Aspect Ratio): Best for square compositions, like those on Instagram.

  L: 16.0 megapixels (4000 x 4000).

  M: 7.1 megapixels (2656 x 2656).

  S1: 3.9 megapixels (1984 x 1984).

  S2: 2.6 megapixels (1600 x 1600).

4. Folder Management

- New Folders: Users can create and select new folders for organizing images directly in-camera. This feature is particularly useful for separating shots from different events or sessions.

5. File Numbering

The R100 offers three options for file numbering, helping photographers maintain an organized workflow:

- Continuous: Numbers files sequentially, even when changing folders or memory cards.
- Auto Reset: Resets numbering when a new folder is created or a new card is inserted.
- Manual Reset: Allows users to reset file numbering manually at any time.

Applications and Benefits

1. Professional Editing: RAW and C-RAW formats provide maximum image data for detailed post-processing.
2. Storage Optimization: C-RAW files save space while retaining high quality, and JPEG compression levels offer additional flexibility.
3. Versatile Resolutions: Multiple aspect ratios and resolutions accommodate different creative needs, from large prints to quick social media uploads.
4. Easy Organization: Folder management and customizable file numbering streamline workflow for event and project photographers.

EOS MOVIE CAPABILITIES

The Canon EOS R100 delivers a versatile set of movie recording features, allowing users to capture high-quality videos in various resolutions and frame rates. Below is an in-depth breakdown of its video capabilities:

1. Movie Type
- Format: MP4
- Compression: MPEG-4 AVC/H.264 for video and AAC for audio. This ensures efficient compression and compatibility with most playback and editing software.

2. Movie Sizes and Frame Rates
The EOS R100 supports multiple resolutions and frame rates, catering to different creative needs:
- 4K UHD (3840 x 2160):
Frame Rates: 23.98 / 25 fps
Compression: IPB (Standard)
Audio: AAC
High resolution is ideal for cinematic-quality videos and detailed visuals.
- Full HD (1920 x 1080):
Frame Rates: 59.94 / 50 / 29.97 / 25 / 23.98 fps
Compression: IPB (Standard)
Audio: AAC
Versatile resolution for most video projects, offering smoother motion at higher frame rates.
- HD (1280 x 720):
Frame Rates: 59.94 / 50 fps
Compression: IPB (Standard)
Audio: AAC
Suitable for web content or scenarios where smaller file sizes are preferred.
- High Frame Rate (HFR) Movies:
Resolution: 1280 x 720
Frame Rates: 119.88 / 100 fps

Compression: IPB (Standard)

No audio recorded; outputs slow-motion movies at 1/4 speed for dramatic effects.

- Time-Lapse Movies:

Resolutions: 4K UHD (3840 x 2160) / Full HD (1920 x 1080)

Frame Rates: 29.97 / 25 fps

Compression: ALL-I

No audio recorded; perfect for capturing gradual changes over time, like sunsets or cityscapes.

- Miniature Effect Movies:

Resolution: Full HD (1920 x 1080)

Frame Rates: 29.97 / 25 / 23.98 fps

Compression: IPB (Standard)

No audio recorded; creates a tilt-shift effect for creative storytelling.

3. Color Sampling

- 4K / Full HD: YCbCr 4:2:0, 8-bit.

While sufficient for most users, it lacks the higher bit-depth and color sampling required for advanced color grading.

4. Canon Log

- Not supported: The absence of Canon Log limits dynamic range enhancements and advanced grading capabilities in post-production.

5. Movie Length

- Maximum duration: 29 minutes, 59 seconds per clip.
- Maximum file sizes:

SDXC (exFAT): Unlimited (practical size depends on card capacity).

SDHC (FAT32): 4 GB per file.

SD (FAT16/FAT12): 2 GB per file.

6. High Frame Rate Movies

- Resolution: 1280 x 720
- Frame Rates: 100 or 119.88 fps

- Outputs slow-motion footage at 1/4 speed, ideal for sports or dramatic sequences.

7. Frame Grab

The camera allows users to extract 8.3-megapixel JPEG stills from 4K UHD videos, offering flexibility for capturing high-resolution moments from recorded footage.

8. Bitrate

Video bitrates vary depending on resolution and frame rate:

- 4K UHD (23.98/25 fps): 120 Mbps (IPB).
- Full HD (59.94/50 fps): 60 Mbps (IPB).
- Full HD (29.97/23.98/25 fps): 30 Mbps (IPB).
- HD (59.94/50 fps): 26 Mbps (IPB).
- HFR Movies: 52 Mbps (IPB).
- 4K Time-Lapse (29.97/25 fps): 300 Mbps (ALL-I).
- Full HD Time-Lapse (29.97/25 fps): 90 Mbps (ALL-I).
- Miniature Effect Movies: 30 Mbps (IPB).

9. Audio

- Built-in monaural microphone:
  Sampling Rate: 48 KHz.
  Bit Depth: 16-bit, 2 channels.
- External microphone input is not supported.

10. HDMI Display and Output

- HDMI Micro OUT Terminal (Type D):
  Allows output to external monitors.
  Supports resolutions:
  4K (UHD): NTSC (23.98 fps), PAL (25.00 fps).
  Full HD (1080): NTSC (59.94p/59.94i), PAL (50.00p/50.00i).
  HD (720p) and Standard Definition also supported.

HDMI output does not record to the camera when connected to an external recorder, but displays shooting information.

. Focusing for Video

- 4K: Uses contrast detection AF, which may be slower than other modes.
- Full HD: Leverages Canon's Dual Pixel CMOS AF, offering smooth and accurate autofocus for video.
- HFR Movies: Autofocus is disabled, requiring manual focus adjustments.

12. ISO for Movies

- Auto ISO: Range of 100–12,800, expandable to H: 25,600.
- Manual ISO: Range of 100–12,800, expandable to H: 25,600.
- This flexibility ensures proper exposure in varying lighting conditions, from bright daylight to low-light environments.

13. Dual Card Recording

- Not supported: The EOS R100 does not allow simultaneous recording to two memory cards, limiting redundancy options.

Applications and Benefits

1. 4K Recording: Perfect for detailed and cinematic-quality videos.
2. Slow Motion: High frame rate options allow for smooth slow-motion effects in HD.
3. Time-Lapse: Offers built-in time-lapse functionality in both 4K and Full HD resolutions.
4. Frame Grabs: Provides an easy way to extract stills from video footage, adding versatility to your content creation.
5. Compact Video Solution: Built-in microphone and HDMI output ensure streamlined functionality for casual and entry-level videographers.

OTHER FEATURES

The Canon EOS R100 is equipped with additional features that enhance usability, customization, and functionality, making it a well-rounded camera for both beginners and advanced users. Below is a detailed breakdown of its other features:

1. Custom Functions
The EOS R100 offers a range of customizable options to suit individual shooting preferences:
- ISO Expansion: Enables expanded ISO settings for challenging lighting conditions.
- Safety Shift: Automatically adjusts settings (aperture, shutter speed, or ISO) to maintain proper exposure in difficult lighting.
- Customizable Buttons: Up to 7 buttons can be customized for easy access to frequently used functions:
  Shutter button (half-press for focus and metering).
  Exposure compensation button.
  AE lock button.
  ISO speed setting button.
  Flash button.
  Movie shooting button.
  Drive mode button.
- Release Shutter Without Lens: Allows the camera to operate even when no lens is attached, useful for certain adapters or creative setups.
- Retract Lens on Power Off: Automatically retracts the lens when the camera is turned off (if the lens supports this feature).

2. Metadata Tagging
The camera includes features to embed metadata into image files for better organization and copyright protection:
- User Copyright Information: Users can input their author's name and copyright details to tag their images.
- Image Rating: Rate images from 0 to 5 stars, simplifying post-shooting organization and selection.

3. LCD Panel / Illumination
- Not Included: The EOS R100 does not feature a top-mounted LCD panel for displaying camera settings or illumination.

4. Water/Dust Resistance
- Not Weather-Sealed: The camera does not include water or dust resistance, so it is not suitable for extreme weather or rugged environments.

5. Voice Memo
- Not Supported: The EOS R100 does not have voice memo functionality for adding audio notes to images.

6. Intelligent Orientation Sensor
- Not Included: The camera does not automatically detect and record the orientation of images during shooting.

7. Playback Features
- Playback Zoom: Magnify images from 1.5x to 10x in 15 levels, making it easier to review focus and detail.
- Display Formats:
  Single image with information (toggleable options).
  Single image without additional data.
  Index display of 4, 9, 36, or 100 images.
- SlideShow Options:
  Playback time options: 1, 2, 3, 5, 10, or 20 seconds.
  Repeat: Enable or disable.
  Transition effects: Choose from Off, Slide in (1-2), or Fade (1-3).
  Background music: On/Off (music must be added via the Camera Connect app or EOS Utility).

Histogram and Highlight Alert
- Histogram: Available for both brightness and RGB color channels, helping evaluate exposure and color balance.
- Highlight Alert: Identifies overexposed areas in an image by flashing highlights during playback.

9. Image Erase and Protection
- Image Erase:

  Options: Single image, selected range, selected images, folder, card, or all found images.
- Image Erase Protection:

  Protect images to prevent accidental deletion:

  Protect single images, selected ranges, or all images in a folder.

10. Self-Timer
- Options:

  2 seconds: Useful for reducing camera shake during long exposures or macro shots.

  10 seconds: Ideal for group shots or self-portraits.

11. Menu Categories
The EOS R100's menu system is intuitive and well-organized, offering six categories:
1. Shooting Menu: Access shooting-related settings and controls.
2. Playback Menu: Manage playback options, such as image review and editing.
3. Communication Features Menu: Adjust Wi-Fi and Bluetooth settings for file transfer and remote control.
4. Function Settings Menu: Customize camera functions and preferences.
5. Display Level Settings Menu: Adjust on-screen display settings.
6. My Menu: Personalize frequently used settings for quick access.

12. Menu Languages
The EOS R100 supports 29 languages, making it accessible to users worldwide. Supported languages include:

- English, German, French, Dutch, Danish, Portuguese, Finnish, Italian, Norwegian, Swedish, Spanish, Greek, Russian, Polish, Czech, Hungarian, Romanian, Ukrainian, Turkish, Arabic, Thai, Simplified Chinese, Traditional Chinese, Korean, Malay, Vietnamese, Indonesian, Hindi, and Japanese.

13. Firmware Update

The camera allows users to perform firmware updates via:
- SD Card: Load firmware onto an SD card and update the camera directly.
- EOS Utility: Connect the camera to a computer to update firmware using Canon's software.
- Camera Connect App: Update firmware wirelessly through Canon's mobile app.

Applications and Benefits
1. Customization: The customizable buttons and metadata tagging make the R100 adaptable to different workflows and shooting styles.
2. Playback Versatility: Comprehensive playback options allow for detailed review and quick organization of images.
3. Intuitive Menus: The well-structured menu system and multi-language support ensure ease of use for photographers worldwide.
4. Firmware Updates: User-friendly firmware updating keeps the camera up-to-date with the latest features and fixes.

Custom Functions

The EOS R100 offers a range of customizable options to suit individual shooting preferences:

- ISO Expansion: Enables expanded ISO settings for challenging lighting conditions.
- Safety Shift: Automatically adjusts settings (aperture, shutter speed, or ISO) to maintain proper exposure in difficult lighting.
- Customizable Buttons: Up to 7 buttons can be customized for easy access to frequently used functions:

  Shutter button (half-press for focus and metering).

  Exposure compensation button.

  AE lock button.

  ISO speed setting button.

  Flash button.

  Movie shooting button.

  Drive mode button.
- Release Shutter Without Lens: Allows the camera to operate even when no lens is attached, useful for certain adapters or creative setups.
- Retract Lens on Power Off: Automatically retracts the lens when the camera is turned off (if the lens supports this feature).

2. Metadata Tagging

The camera includes features to embed metadata into image files for better organization and copyright protection:

- User Copyright Information: Users can input their author's name and copyright details to tag their images.
- Image Rating: Rate images from 0 to 5 stars, simplifying post-shooting organization and selection.

3. LCD Panel / Illumination

- Not Included: The EOS R100 does not feature a top-mounted LCD panel for displaying camera settings or illumination.

5. Voice Memo
- Not Supported: The EOS R100 does not have voice memo functionality for adding audio notes to images.

6. Intelligent Orientation Sensor
- Not Included: The camera does not automatically detect and record the orientation of images during shooting.

7. Playback Features
- Playback Zoom: Magnify images from 1.5x to 10x in 15 levels, making it easier to review focus and detail.
- Display Formats:
  Single image with information (toggleable options).
  Single image without additional data.
  Index display of 4, 9, 36, or 100 images.
- SlideShow Options:
  Playback time options: 1, 2, 3, 5, 10, or 20 seconds.
  Repeat: Enable or disable.
  Transition effects: Choose from Off, Slide in (1-2), or Fade (1-3).
  Background music: On/Off (music must be added via the Camera Connect app or EOS Utility).

8. Histogram and Highlight Alert
- Histogram: Available for both brightness and RGB color channels, helping evaluate exposure and color balance.
- Highlight Alert: Identifies overexposed areas in an image by flashing highlights during playback.

9. Image Erase and Protection
- Image Erase:
  Options: Single image, selected range, selected images, folder, card, or all found images.

- Image Erase Protection:

Protect images to prevent accidental deletion:

Protect single images, selected ranges, or all images in a folder.

10. Self-Timer

- Options:

2 seconds: Useful for reducing camera shake during long exposures or macro shots.

10 seconds: Ideal for group shots or self-portraits.

11. Menu Categories

The EOS R100's menu system is intuitive and well-organized, offering six categories:

1. Shooting Menu: Access shooting-related settings and controls.
2. Playback Menu: Manage playback options, such as image review and editing.
3. Communication Features Menu: Adjust Wi-Fi and Bluetooth settings for file transfer and remote control.
4. Function Settings Menu: Customize camera functions and preferences.
5. Display Level Settings Menu: Adjust on-screen display settings.
6. My Menu: Personalize frequently used settings for quick access.

12. Menu Languages

The EOS R100 supports 29 languages, making it accessible to users worldwide. Supported languages include:

- English, German, French, Dutch, Danish, Portuguese, Finnish, Italian, Norwegian, Swedish, Spanish, Greek, Russian, Polish, Czech, Hungarian, Romanian, Ukrainian, Turkish, Arabic, Thai, Simplified Chinese, Traditional Chinese, Korean, Malay, Vietnamese, Indonesian, Hindi, and Japanese.

13. Firmware Update

The camera allows users to perform firmware updates via:

- SD Card: Load firmware onto an SD card and update the camera directly.

OTHER FEATURES

- EOS Utility: Connect the camera to a computer to update firmware using Canon's software.
- Camera Connect App: Update firmware wirelessly through Canon's mobile app.

Applications and Benefits

1. Customization: The customizable buttons and metadata tagging make the R100 adaptable to different workflows and shooting styles.
2. Playback Versatility: Comprehensive playback options allow for detailed review and quick organization of images.
3. Intuitive Menus: The well-structured menu system and multi-language support ensure ease of use for photographers worldwide.
4. Firmware Updates: User-friendly firmware updating keeps the camera up-to-date with the latest features and fixes.

INTERFACE

The Canon EOS R100 is equipped with a range of connectivity and interface options, enabling seamless communication with other devices and accessories. Here's a detailed breakdown of its interface features:

1. Computer Connectivity
 • Hi-Speed USB (USB 2.0):
 The camera uses a USB Type-C terminal for wired connections to a computer.
 Ideal for transferring files or tethered shooting using Canon's EOS Utility software.
 Although it supports USB 2.0, it lacks the higher speeds of USB 3.0 or 3.1, which may result in slower transfer rates for large files.

2. Wi-Fi Connectivity
 • Wireless LAN (IEEE 802.11b/g/n):
 Operates on the 2.4 GHz band, ensuring compatibility with most Wi-Fi networks.
 Supports the following features:
    EOS Utility: Allows for remote shooting and file transfers from the camera to a computer.
    Smartphone Connectivity: Use Canon's Camera Connect App to transfer images, control the camera remotely, or add GPS data via a paired smartphone.
    Upload to image.canon: Enables direct uploads to Canon's cloud storage platform for easy backup and sharing.
    Wireless Printing: Compatible with Wi-Fi-enabled printers for direct printing of images.
    Bluetooth 4.2:
 Provides low-energy connectivity for maintaining a continuous link with a smartphone or tablet.
 Useful for remote control, geotagging, or initiating Wi-Fi connections quickly.

3. HDMI Output
- Micro HDMI (Type-D Connector):
Allows output to external displays or recorders.

Supports HDR output to compatible TVs, enabling enhanced dynamic range for playback.

Note: Recording via HDMI output is not possible while simultaneously recording to the camera.

4. External Microphone Support
- 3.5mm Stereo Mini Jack:
Provides an input for connecting external microphones, improving audio quality for video recording.

Offers greater flexibility for vloggers, interviewers, or content creators requiring high-quality sound.

Applications and Benefits
1. Flexible Connectivity: The combination of USB, Wi-Fi, and Bluetooth ensures easy integration with computers, smartphones, and other devices.
2. Enhanced Video Output: The HDMI output allows for HDR playback or use with external monitors for detailed viewing and composition.
3. Improved Audio Quality: External microphone support enhances audio capture for professional video projects.
4. Convenience: Wireless printing and cloud uploads simplify workflows by reducing dependency on physical storage or manual transfers.

DIRECT PRINT CAPABILITIES

The Canon EOS R100 offers direct printing features, allowing users to print photos without the need for a computer. Below is a detailed breakdown of its direct print capabilities:

1. Compatibility with Canon Printers
The EOS R100 is designed to work seamlessly with compatible Canon printers, including:
- Canon Compact Photo Printers: Ideal for quick, high-quality prints of smaller photo sizes, such as 4x6-inch prints.
- Canon PIXMA Printers: Supports larger print sizes and additional printing features like borderless printing and color enhancements.

2. PictBridge Support
- PictBridge Compatibility:

The camera supports PictBridge, a standard for direct printing from cameras to printers without a computer.

It is compatible with wireless LAN PictBridge-enabled printers, allowing users to print photos wirelessly.

Applications and Benefits
1. Quick and Convenient Printing: Direct printing eliminates the need for transferring files to a computer, enabling fast and easy production of physical prints.
2. Wireless Printing: PictBridge over Wi-Fi simplifies the printing process, allowing users to connect directly to compatible printers without cables.
3. Seamless Canon Ecosystem: Integration with Canon printers ensures optimal print quality and compatibility with Canon-specific features like borderless printing.

STORAGE

The Canon EOS R100 uses standard memory card storage to save photos and videos. Here's a detailed breakdown of its storage capabilities:

1. Storage Type
The EOS R100 supports the following memory card formats:
- SD (Secure Digital): Standard memory card format for basic storage needs.
- SDHC (Secure Digital High Capacity): Supports higher storage capacities, up to 32 GB, ideal for users requiring more space for high-resolution images and Full HD videos.
- SDXC (Secure Digital Extended Capacity): Offers capacities of 64 GB and beyond, making it suitable for 4K video recording and large numbers of high-resolution photos.

2. UHS-I Compatibility
- The camera is compatible with UHS-I (Ultra High Speed) cards, which provide faster read and write speeds than standard SD cards.
- This ensures smooth performance for continuous shooting, 4K video recording, and quick file transfers.

Applications and Benefits
1. Flexible Storage Options: The compatibility with SD, SDHC, and SDXC cards ensures users can choose the right storage capacity for their needs, from casual photography to intensive video projects.
2. High-Speed Performance: UHS-I support enhances shooting efficiency by reducing buffering during continuous shooting and enabling smoother video recording.
3. Expandable Capacity: SDXC compatibility allows users to store large files, such as 4K videos and RAW images, without worrying about running out of space.

SUPPORTED OPERATING SYSTEMS

The Canon EOS R100 is compatible with both PC and Macintosh platforms, ensuring users can seamlessly transfer and manage their images and videos across popular operating systems.

1. PC (Windows)
The camera supports the following Windows operating systems:
- Windows 10 (64-bit): Compatible with all current Canon software and utilities, such as EOS Utility, Digital Photo Professional (DPP), and Camera Connect.
- Windows 11 (64-bit): Full compatibility with Canon's latest drivers and software for transferring files, remote shooting, and post-processing.

2. Macintosh (Mac)
The EOS R100 supports macOS, including:
- macOS 11 Big Sur and later: Works seamlessly with Canon's software suite for macOS.
- Apple Silicon (M1 and M2 Chips): Fully compatible with Canon applications optimized for the new generation of Mac hardware.
- macOS Ventura (latest release): Ensures support for Canon's ecosystem, including wireless file transfers and tethered shooting.

Applications and Benefits
1. Cross-Platform Compatibility: Works with both Windows and macOS, allowing flexibility for users across different ecosystems.
2. Seamless Integration: Canon's software, such as EOS Utility and DPP, supports these operating systems for tethered shooting, firmware updates, and advanced image processing.

The Canon EOS R100 is supported by a suite of software tools and apps that enhance its functionality, streamline workflows, and offer advanced editing options. Here's a breakdown of the software available for the EOS R100:

1. Image Processing
- Digital Photo Professional (DPP):

Canon's dedicated software for processing and editing RAW and JPEG files.

Offers advanced tools for adjusting exposure, white balance, tone curves, noise reduction, and lens corrections.

Supports batch processing for efficient workflows.

Compatible with Canon's Digital Lens Optimizer (DLO) for correcting lens aberrations and maximizing image quality.

2. Other Software
- Picture Style Editor:

Allows users to create and customize their own Picture Styles to achieve specific looks and tonal effects.

Provides flexibility for photographers seeking a unique visual identity in their images.
- EOS Utility:

Essential software for tethered shooting and camera control.

Enables remote shooting and live view operation from a computer.

Simplifies firmware updates and file transfers to a PC or Mac.
- Image Transfer Utility:

Automates the transfer of images from the camera to a computer or cloud service.

Works in conjunction with Canon's image.canon platform for seamless backup and sharing.

3. Camera Connect App
- Platform Availability:

Compatible with both iOS and Android devices.

Features:

Wireless file transfer: Quickly transfer images and videos to a smartphone or tablet.

Remote shooting: Control the camera, adjust settings, and trigger the shutter remotely.

GPS Tagging: Use your smartphone's GPS to add location data to your photos.

Firmware updates: Check for and install firmware updates wirelessly.

Applications and Benefits

- Advanced Editing: With DPP and Picture Style Editor, users can fine-tune their images for professional results.
- Seamless Connectivity: EOS Utility and Image Transfer Utility simplify workflows for photographers working across devices.
- Mobile Flexibility: The Camera Connect app enhances the camera's wireless functionality, enabling on-the-go transfers and remote control.

POWER SOURCE

The Canon EOS R100 is designed to offer efficient and reliable power management, ensuring optimal performance for both still photography and video recording. Here's a breakdown of its power source and related features:

1. Batteries
- The EOS R100 is powered by a single rechargeable Li-ion Battery LP-E17.

Lightweight and compact, the LP-E17 ensures portability and ease of use.

Compatible with other Canon cameras using the same battery type, making it convenient for users who already own Canon gear.

2. Battery Life
The battery life of the EOS R100 varies based on usage mode (measured using a fully charged LP-E17 and CIPA standards):
- Viewfinder Usage: Approximately 340 shots per charge.
- Live View Usage: Approximately 430 shots per charge, offering a longer runtime compared to using the viewfinder.
- 4K Movie Recording: Approximately 110 minutes of continuous recording.
- Full HD Movie Recording: Approximately 160 minutes of continuous recording.
- Playback Time: When playing a slideshow of still images, the battery lasts for approximately 190 minutes.

These numbers make the R100 suitable for moderate-length photo sessions and video projects, though additional batteries may be required for extended use.

3. Battery Indicator
The camera features a 4-level battery indicator, which provides real-time updates on battery life:
1. Full charge
2. Three-quarters
3. Half charge

- Low battery

This helps users manage their shooting sessions effectively by monitoring the remaining power.

4. Power Saving Features

The EOS R100 includes several power-saving options to extend battery life:

- Display Off Timer: Automatically turns off the display after 15, 30 seconds, or 1, 3, 5, 10, or 30 minutes of inactivity.
- Auto Power Down: Shuts down the camera after 30 seconds or 1, 3, 5, or 10 minutes of inactivity (can also be disabled if desired).
- Viewfinder Off Timer: Automatically powers down the viewfinder after 1 or 3 minutes of inactivity (can also be disabled).
- Power Saving Mode: Adjusts settings to conserve power during extended usage.

5. Power Supply and Battery Chargers

The EOS R100 supports a variety of power supply options for flexibility:

- Battery Charger LC-E17E:

  A compact charger designed for recharging the LP-E17 battery.

  Ideal for both at-home and on-the-go charging.

- AC Adapter AC-E6N:

Allows the camera to be powered via an electrical outlet for extended use, such as during studio shoots or when capturing time-lapse sequences.

- DC Coupler DR-E18:

  Works with the AC adapter to provide a constant power source, making it suitable for long shooting sessions or video recording without relying on battery life.

Applications and Benefits

1. Extended Shooting: The robust battery life ensures that users can capture hundreds of photos or over an hour of video on a single charge.

POWER SOURCE

- Power Flexibility: Multiple power-saving settings help conserve energy during long sessions.
- Alternative Power Options: The availability of an AC adapter and DC coupler allows for continuous power during demanding tasks like time-lapse photography or lengthy studio shoots.

ACCESSORIES FOR THE CANON EOS R100

The Canon EOS R100 supports a wide range of accessories to enhance its functionality and versatility. From lens adapters to flash systems and remote controllers, the R100 is well-equipped to meet the diverse needs of photographers and videographers. Below is a detailed breakdown of its accessories:

1. Wireless File Transmitter
- Not Compatible: The Canon EOS R100 does not support wireless file transmitters, limiting its compatibility with professional-grade wireless image transfer devices.

2. Cases and Straps
- Protecting Cloths:

  PC-E1: Soft and durable cloth for wrapping and protecting the camera during transport.

  PC-E2: An alternative protecting cloth offering similar functionality.
- Strap: A standard camera strap is included with the EOS R100, ensuring safe handling and ease of carrying.

3. Lenses
The Canon EOS R100 is compatible with a variety of lenses, ensuring flexibility for different photography styles:
- RF and RF-S Lenses:

  Natively supported lenses from Canon's mirrorless RF lineup, offering cutting-edge optical performance and advanced features.
- EF and EF-S Lenses:

  Compatible via a Mount Adapter EF-EOS R, allowing users to use lenses from Canon's DSLR lineup.
- EF-M Lenses:

  Not compatible: EF-M lenses designed for Canon's EOS M series cameras cannot be used with the EOS R100.

4. Lens Adapters
- Mount Adapter EF-EOS R:

  Allows seamless use of Canon EF and EF-S lenses with full functionality, including autofocus and image stabilization.

- Drop-In Filter Mount Adapter EF-EOS R:

Supports the use of drop-in filters, such as ND filters or polarizers, with compatible EF and EF-S lenses.

Flash Systems

The EOS R100 supports a wide range of Canon Speedlite flashes for enhanced lighting options:

- EL Series Speedlites:

EL-1: High-performance flash with advanced features for professional lighting.

EL-100: Compact and versatile flash for everyday use.

- EX Series Speedlites: Compatible with Canon's EX series flashes, including macro-specific options.
- Macrolite: Specialized flashes for close-up and macro photography.
- Speedlite Transmitters:

ST-E3-RT (Ver. 2), ST-E3-RT, and ST-E2: Enable wireless control of multiple Speedlite units for complex lighting setups.

- Off-Camera Shoe Cord OC-E3:

Provides flexibility to position a Speedlite flash off-camera while maintaining full functionality.

6. Remote Controllers and Switches

The EOS R100 supports remote shooting accessories for enhanced control:

- Bluetooth Remote BR-E1:

Allows wireless control of the camera for triggering the shutter or recording videos.

- Tripod Grip HG-100TBR:

A compact tripod grip with an integrated remote, ideal for vlogging and handheld shooting.

- Remote Switch RS-60E3:

A wired remote switch for triggering the shutter without touching the camera, reducing vibrations during long exposures or macro photography.

Other Accessories
- Interface Cables:

IFC-100U and IFC-400U: High-quality cables for connecting the camera to a computer or other devices for file transfer or tethered shooting.

Applications and Benefits
1. Lens Adaptability: The ability to use RF, RF-S, EF, and EF-S lenses with the appropriate adapter ensures versatility for various shooting styles.
2. Advanced Lighting: Compatibility with Canon's Speedlite system, including wireless transmitters, provides extensive lighting options for creative photography.
3. Remote Shooting: The Bluetooth remote and tripod grip enhance convenience for vlogging, group shots, and long exposure photography.
4. Protection and Transport: Protective cloths and the included strap ensure the camera remains safe and easy to handle.

PHYSICAL SPECIFICATIONS

The Canon EOS R100 is designed with a lightweight, compact body while maintaining durability and functionality. Below is a detailed breakdown of its physical specifications:

1. Body Materials

- Construction:

The EOS R100's body is made from polycarbonate resin reinforced with glass fiber, offering a lightweight yet durable structure.

It incorporates aluminum alloy in key areas to enhance rigidity and durability while keeping the overall weight minimal.

- Benefits:

The combination of materials ensures a balance between portability and robustness, making the camera suitable for daily use and travel.

2. Operating Environment

- Temperature Range: Operates within a range of 0 – 40°C, allowing it to perform reliably in a variety of weather conditions, from mild cold to warm environments.
- Humidity: Designed to function in environments with 85% or less humidity, but it is not weather-sealed, so care is needed in extreme weather or high-humidity conditions.

3. Dimensions

- Size (W x H x D): 116.3 x 85.5 x 68.8 mm.

The compact size makes it easy to carry in small camera bags or backpacks, ideal for photographers on the go.

- Benefits:

Its small form factor is particularly useful for travel, street photography, and vloggers seeking portability without compromising image quality.

PHYSICAL SPECIFICATIONS

Weight
- Body Only: Weighs approximately 356 g.

Lightweight construction ensures comfortable handling, even during extended shooting sessions.

With a lens attached, the camera remains manageable for handheld shooting.

Applications and Benefits
1. Portability: The compact size and lightweight design make the EOS R100 perfect for travel, casual shooting, and vloggers seeking a mobile setup.
2. Durability: The polycarbonate resin with glass fiber and aluminum alloy construction provides a solid build that can withstand everyday use.
3. User Comfort: Its lightweight nature reduces fatigue during long shoots, making it a great choice for photographers and videographers alike.